OMBLIGO /

/ INTAGLIO

Vör Götte

Ricochet Editions

Cover art: Nicole Simpkins

Book design by Betsy Medvedovsky
Published by Ricochet Editions
http://ricocheteditions.com

Ricochet titles are distributed by Small Press Distribution.
This title is also available for purchase directly from the publisher
www.spdbooks.org / 800-869-7553

Library of Congress Cataloging-in-Publication Data
OMBLIGO // INTAGLIO / Vör Götte
Library of Congress Control Number 2018959040
Götte, Vör

ISBN-13: 978-1-938900-27-3

FIRST EDITION

If a carver sees the future in a hunk of uncut jade, which is more real, the sculpture. Or the stone that's carved away?

—TESSA RUMSEY

excavation site I :

Can you speak / w/o yr tongue
snapping off in the throat of another? Pear of Anguish, it's springtime

         cranks

                   [TAG 1]

melt

         midwife moon

         ma ma   moo moo

               [TAG 2]
            caul caterwaul aaaaaaaaaarrriaaaaaa

            excavation site II :
Or does a clear thought only follow a question
woman reliquary
        triste, tristes, of stump removal
snap snap
snap snap snap

[TAG 3]
goes the ecstatic

                                        excavation site III :
So the rubble flocks together
                    (sighting: Arctic ptarmigan belly-up in the South Pole)
(remains
            of a heretic chain; *triste, tristes*, relic of the Inquisition)

[TAG 4]
relic / Ye
wandering womb / hear ye

excavation site IV :

puked pearls as small assemblies of prodigal suns   [TAG 5, 6, 7]
                its papal bull / mercury in the veins
                      a little ice age
                      Lobotomizes attachment to another

excavation site V :

snap snap
snap

sites I-V :

BRUISE	(conditions)
AMBER FINGER	(inscription)
GLASS *FATI*	(smoothed)
VOLCANO CLOTHES	(*aporia*)
RAZE/RAISE	(pink habits)

BRUISE _____
          (conditions)

A b-side to a one-sided story; in 1961 my mother was three and not thinking of me

—and why should she;

My mother has something to say, now, to me: *come home to me;*

This call is a bruise; a bruise paling; paling like ice or sand, minerals, petrified wood—the bruise is the expression of delay—understood when the grip stops gripping;

First the pale fingerprint, then blue—does it speak to you? *It speaks to me;*

My mother says *come home* but what she means is *how long will this go on;* how long before telling her my regret over the phone becomes static; how long can a person stand static before it becomes song; what tech will "ferret out 'signals' buried in 'noise'"; and when, and who?

Will a man? Will someone like Richard G. Woodbridge III, ethnomusicologist,

find music embedded in the grooves of ancient dishware by stroking the pots with a needle, as he swore he did in 1961?

A "crystal cartridge," will they sing;

Will stroking the paint of ancient masters with this needle reveal the bruise of their colors, the conditions for their making?

Will bruising my skin with my finger reveal the conditions of my conception?

Archaeoacoustics, he called it; called

The unearthing of music from dead matter; from artifact; as in: its birth minute—

A genetic minute inscribed in the material, as in: the pot remembers its potter

the way I remember my mother in accumulations;

Her voice as I practice saying *Mom, mom;* the trace of voice; I forget how I was made; to think about it is to disassociate;

To hover above my body as if I am not attached to its condition libidinally, or by the imposition of culture which tells me to be grossed out by parental love-making;

Beginning in the question: can we hear the makers making their made-things?

By coaxing the made-things out of their object-sleep—

I watched with glee / while your kings and queens / fought for ten decades / for the gods they made / woo woo woo woo;

Dead ivy scratching; at a window whose pane is paling with frost;

Where this line of questioning leads: is the birth scream of my mother sunk somewhere in my bones—?

If I scratch at thought can I hear her; if I behave as an archeologist, who makes slow and punctuated sweeps at a cochlea cupped in a mass of hard dirt;

Who swept my face with a piece of paper; as I burst from a sac balloon; this caul is a bruise;

A bruise paling like a fated baby;

If I fall in swoons upon procession with the dead will my ghost self speak?

Does the heirloom speak to you? Will she;

Does the process of excavation determine human worthiness—

How to read the undecayed, the underexposed; the amniotic voicing in a grassy underbelly—

Woodbridge, hopeful he'll be remembered; hopeful as varnish, mauve and shellacked; hopeful as those financially backed can rustle time—just enough that he'll be remembered;

In 1961 he swore he heard a word; "'blue,' [which] was located in a blue paint stroke—as if the artist was talking to himself or to the subject," *to the gods they made / blue blue blue blue;*

No one who recreated the experiment had this result.

[TAG 8]

who winters

who stays   in the fray

If I let mutter mother matter, it dates back longer than that;

Since to remember is to fear being forgotten—is the birth scream of my
mother sunk somewhere in my bones?

A trauma lodges itself in the trapezius, *tristeza,* like the Spanish Inquisition
c. 1478, aimed at erasing a history built from ritual, rhythm, choreography;
triste, tristes

Harrowing the dirt; ossified, an object [from Medieval Latin objectum: thing
presented to the mind] heresy is an internal threat; heresy

Says the words without believing them;

Wears a body without feeling it; it "checks out," it is not hungry, it is
autonomic; it zooms out; look—there is someone lodged in the ice?

Since ice preserves what could be eaten later, ice is like devotion; faith
beyond hunger; agriculture beyond famine; art beyond investment; a glacial
moraine scooping up the ground;

A self-pitying nightingale shoving its desire into a register of preemptive
mourning;

Antarctica is the only continent "discovered" by European explorers,
in the sense of the word that includes a body's experience as well as
conceptualizing territory, in space uninhabited up to that point;

Object [from Medieval Latin objectum: thing presented to the mind]

Barrenness; silences beyond scope; certain frozen death; blank page;

*Although we've come to the end of the road / Still I can't let you go / It's
unnatural / you belong to me / I belong to you;* ice is a mineral; hardly still;

But I am—I dwell in the abstract—I think of my mother who has declared
herself *not a poetry person;* I think of pop songs like earworms trailing from
a musical corpus;

Eons ago, that was eons ago;

I think of ice, how it is colorless unless flawed and cracked; bacteria bloat
beneath the surface;

On the surface, bacteria cannot survive their conditions; the sea teems with
unnamable species;

And divers call this engorging "The Cathedral;" in *Encounters at the End of the World,* Werner Herzog calls them "priests, preparing for mass;" they call the experience "holy;"

Maybe I was snowblind / but it seemed the wind spoke true / and I believed its stories then / as dreamers often do / in Antarctica.

The surface is not as it seems; sastrugi erect themselves like an army of scorpions over the snow—but I do not—I call my writing weeping lemon meringue; it's sweeter;

Herzog then asks, "is there such a thing as insanity amongst penguins?" As a choir soundtrack swells in the background, a fleeing penguin is filmed with his wings out wide; "this penguin is already 80 kilometers from where it should be...headed toward the interior of the continent...5000 kilometers ahead of him...let him go."

White void; certain death; certain bruising toward death or color?

Electric fishes a false moon; yes yes *triste tristes;* to follow when the real one leads to death;

Clumsy as loneliness for one who has stuck themself away from a society which might force them to speak, and has discovered there is not much that really *needs* to be said, not because it's been said already, but because chatter is a waste of gas;

Stare at the snow long enough, maybe forever, it slows you down:

Jason Anthony, who has spent eight seasons there working as part of the U.S.'s Antarctica Program, discusses snow color, "Now I know: white is blue. Antarctica is not white. Look closely at the snow at your feet, even more closely at the snow out beyond. Where I say white, think pale reflected grays and incremental blues. When you ask which blue, think bruise behind lace. When you think hue, think oblivion."

Anchorite tourmaline is found on every continent; it means "colorless;"

Like a chalk outline of a body on pavement; body tags marking the spot for forensic excavation; how cruel of the ice to preserve the flesh that wants to escape it.

Waste; coloration; a bruise is how many colors of human desire; a bruise is a
long raceme of failure to speak; adamantine spar;

Under these conditions one may choose to armor herself in Siberian bear-
hunting gear, so that the spikes turn outward; one becomes an urchin of the
tundra;

A blank page breeds an armored specimen fearful of dying by what she
hunts; something of the food chain here;

Help is never on the way when a child desires to rub the image of herself on
the rock; when a midwife rubs her caul on a page; this call is a bruise;

Pages are threatened by the act that keeps them alive; thumbing; thumbing
to stay alive; reading the Running element;

I am caught between being an urchin-bear hunter and a hunter of pages;
huntress under the moon; dying for the blank page;

Dying, for the blank page is a water kingdom; quarry from which or(e) & the
oxygen;

Or gold may be extracted; a reservoir in conceptual territory;

To think of writing as food; not desire for food; to think of writing as
process; a sacrifice of living for the backward gesture of its capitulation;

(to See to See to Breathe(; page turns to ice(seasoning;

a problem(; forgotten; writing is a bioengineered technology; writing is a
problem;

of variegation; of translation; of textiles;

of posthumous salve for the failure to speak; making time arbitrary; eons,
that was eons ago;

She asks herself, when you clothe a monolith, does it become an emperor or
a saboteur?

Each is a machine in a machine;

Destined to make imitations of grand origins, like a poet; her allegiance to
ephemera while spitting up matter; minerals; vitamins;

We may be better off)cold color in the either; space between ruination and
Oh let's save

The (ruin(chopped up quartzite boulder;

the writing is synesthesia; a floating; high on a liquid of forgotten
metaphors; cold otherworld bruising; with one
Crack(ing) down my middle; (the otherworld I mean; apophyllite with one)
crack(ing);
I spread my yellow wound toward untoward shores & did not die; (nor) give
up
The crumble(surrounding color must be neutralized for a neutral color to
Color);
to go back to blue;
I am not sad for the matter that assembles itself beneath hard dirt;
Under the archeological sheet like a memory under mental illness; an
earworm;
But I am jealous of the dead, who are exempt from agony; I writhe under a
white sheet;
Combinatory elements assemble themselves in terms of stakes: in terms of
what
You hear v. What you imagine you hear; like using a cyanoscope to measure
the blue in the sky; a blip; the lifespan of the human in the geologic; an
ekphrastic life; afterthought of artifice/experience;
I respond to what I can't experience in body
By inhabiting its image; a consecration; like the relationship of the desert
and the sea;
One is the drained, dry version of the other, an evaporated version, a sand
castle built by the bully of the tides; the other;
The sea itself is fullness, accumulation, all life in hiding; the sea bullies its
cartographers, and v.v.

[TAG 9]

    diagnosis; prognosis; gnosis; amniocentisis ashes ashes

[TAG 10]

    where is joy in a sac balloon; hot air

I mean to say: the material conditions for the flesh are unbearable and
writing is medicine? Okay, medicine;

For those attached to their own devastation, the promise of remaining on
earth forever in the mercury shape of a bog person is a type of recursive
torture;

(Done with blue for now; the bruise turns green; dioptase; jade; emerald);

ow ow ow ow; the promise that millennials may be the first generation *not
to have to die;*

That the body might stay put despite a desire to flee; the cruelty of ice as a
salve for burning the roof of your mouth; for a clumsiness-toward-death;

If medicine ensures immortality, raises the dead; if sinna sinna in da mirral;
qué será será;

At the moment of recognition, this devastation is a forest fire; it looks like it
needs to be put out, but is actually a method of regeneration; restitching;

Object [from Medieval Latin objectum: thing presented to the mind]

I explain to my shadow: conditions are not self-generating limbs; they are
swallowed—a society is a hot box;

But it is no use; I write her a letter from my box—my urchin-armor whose
spikes have curled in on themselves like a fig synconium and I its wasp,
eating myself out;

I look down from an observation tower: at eel pools made to simulate the
Sargasso Sea;

A similar confusion of hatched turtles paddling toward what they think is
the moon;

And I wonder about allowing myself to be covered in leeches, stung by bees,
to purify the blood—

We want to cut them—we want to cut me—out of this picture; in two; false
moon;

Like a worm's bifurcation—a child's chopping it in two on the sidewalk as

---

1   altered from a comic by Harry Hambley, Ketnipz comics.

a type of fascistic order to *play it cool* in body, maintaining the look of a live thing while an emotional life eats her out from the inside;
Like the fungus *Aaspergillus tubingensis*, which chews through polyurethane plastics;
It will likely be bioengineered to eat human garbage;
In this body I thought I wanted to be conquered; wilderness left open to razing; muse;
But the commitment to anonymity became a commitment to incorruptibility;
Carrying the unwanted to term;
A saintly assumption that the life I was permitted was not the one intended by the metaphysicians, who diagnosed me with common language;
Now I am my own little god; straight lines itch; ow ow ow ow;
As I crawl out of the fig by swallowing the fruit flesh I call my conditions I have no place to shit;
I wonder why I have to crawl out of this fig only to burrow myself in another?
I scratch the inside, a crystal cartridge; I am nowhere in Antarctica, the frontier;
but I erase, by way of revision, the shame for having been at its mercy; to revise (to re-see) is to clone myself, becoming double; translating myself, recreating conditions for pain, and rebirth: memory;
Now I am my own little mother; she disapproves of my fear of doppelgängers, my limbless torso, while I loop back to the laboratory;
I tell her the criminal always returns to the scene of the crime, to witness one's own degradation;
The salt-mother shakes her head; who loves like that? She asks; don't you know what it's like hear ice crack as you are walking out of your fish house?

[TAG 11]

fat spillage all across the microscope slide

~~~~~~~~~~no?~~no no~

as if the wind could fill in the eggs I'm lying

Ice accumulates, devotion stands in for heat; *inhaling polyurethane plastics;*
Frost swills in the knobs of the ice house walls;
The gesture of accumulation is comforting, like eating in front of the TV;
While metonymic descriptions, whether image or anecdotal, pile up;
Knowledge is not something *out there;* it is something shared; it is mimetic
cumulus clouds, testimonies; headbanging along with the rest; hoarding
things that already resemble me; hoarding things until they take on my
appearance; specific colors; patterns; threads;
Eating till fullness is no longer a stutter in a never-ending chain of meals
and waiting for them; retail-therapy;
Writing the thought becomes taxonomy of muscular tensions; pinching fat;
I know *you are what you eat,* and food is defined by tastes, or their
occasional interruptions: less flow, more a bulldozer churning up garbage,
then suddenly—!
Like, a raccoon standing there; a not-I;
Or: the engine sputters out; music scratched along the bowl bottoms out;
It becomes obvious I am making it all up; I return to the dumpster;
It snows for a great length of time, maybe forever, and in which case the
change in weather comes as a surprise;
I am no longer describing a radical practice, instead I describe adaptations,
a subtle shift in molecular structure;
The degree by which iridescence reflects the sun's in a polished saxophone;
I consume the space that surrounds me, I consume it as I consume, but do
not pay attention to the phrase, *less is more;*
Because I desire to accumulate and cannot afford to value asceticism;
I cannot call this space a subtle body, diamond body, true and genuine
body, rainbow body, light body, bliss body or immortal; I cannot reduce it
to *habitus, locality, proxemics, dwelling,* or any other category that seeks to
define a person by a particular context, to entrap her in tiers of pixelated
invisibilia so that no person will ever wonder if her being, however deviant,
was ever accidental;
A personal bubble; heresy's internal threat; amniotic voicing;

Whereas external threats against a page: interrupted, invaded—by ink—
conquistadores, oil spills, death squads, burglars, house fires, the U.S. Army,
forced exile, gang rape, ambush—are trauma's further distillation into
simple interactions with other bubbles;
So that even noise is a kind of pain for the hypervigilant, because the injury
reverberates, like sound waves, through the spaces;
It makes sense that the gesture of accumulation is not one of gathering
toward oneself, to build a skyscraper of traumas as if to replicate a Cyclops
of interiority; rather, to ping antennae.

[TAG 12]

reading   Alphabet
                     transacted upon groups of muscles
muscles
Contracted in amber, with the ice, some archive, hard dirt, etc.,
                     Bowl of music / scratched hard enough
          essay in shards / lyric flayed

                 along time scrunched along
                          all along

AMBER FINGER _____
(inscription)

And suppose the ping is dealt with as a matter of dissection, as of a corpse in
Italy in 1543;

a bone misplaced in a body, thrashing under conditions that cannot be
vivisected nor changed;

Teratoma bores itself into the muscles; refugee of hair, debris;

His whole body is a foreign body, invasive species; his whole body;

Is paper—unpeels from a book's spine like muscle from the skeletons in
the Vesalius engravings *de humani corporis fabrica libri septem,* or *de
dissectione partium corporis* by Charles Estienne c. 1545, whose anatomical
representations of skinless bodies writhe in various states of undress;
mannerism;

For instance a man, gutted, buckling under a noose, marionetting the flesh
from his arms;

Has been spreading lies—doomed heretical—filleted to remind him what
danger to purge;

The story is indiscriminate; social;

Discourse set up against practitioners of opaque ecstatic states;

I make a connection to the flesh I am writing—what acts on it is
indiscriminate; social; it gets dug up like a toxic tuber and comes out like
this:

I write the way I feel everything at once; I write the way I see everything at
once; does this make me a solipsist?

The solipsist perhaps grew up like a tuber in a garden seeded by errant
breezes that must beg for water by learning to measure patterns of errancy;

At least the solipsist is honest, R said once about philosophers, implying that
all philosophy is solipsism until challenged on this point;

Medical futurism; medieval retrospection in terms of becoming inured to
spilled guts; private spectacles of pain more palatable than public tortures of
apostatic converts; did I know that I might bleed, saying it?

Does a bruise, as it heals, make a body more or less legible to the general
public; is the point to be seen?

The point of forensics is determining whether the bruises on dirty bones have historic value;

If a bone shows the tenderness of popcorn; if the body was tender as one
eating popcorn; if she ate popcorn;

Man created in image; pages like elderly hands; the dark chrome of artificial,
technological promises;

If instead R had made shadow puppets on the wall, treating human
encounter as such, instead of burying his gaze in his phone, his laptop, his
virtuality;

If instead I'd stopped thinking of life as a matter-puppet for poems;

That our parts might be stitched by light or shadow—or would I have
bled then? Would I have been more honest? Would my oops-garden bleed
the blooms of sprouted tubers or wilder dandelion? The deletion and
disappearance of one;

Glassed—what is fleshy?

In Ethiopian healing scrolls; the encased relic of a saint's hands; the bones of
extinct fish; illegible sacred texts; precious lapis; microfilm; dead languages
and the dented Quonset;

What is more real...?

Object [from Medieval Latin objectum: thing presented to the mind]
A Renaissance perspective drawing that makes certain there is distance
between the viewer and a long point in the background, while in the
foreground, a tiny herd of men argues under a cathedral's luminescent
canopy?

Or the grave-robbed cadaver spread out across the table, unbeaten
heart fished out of the ribs; *putrefy putrefy;* triste, tristes; volcanic axis;
transubstantiated host; bread; to eat Him;

Says the good heretic is a dead heretic; she deserves a spanking;

Would rather this than press the leaves of her life between pages.

[TAG 13]

Ye have little / scrunched along the mustard rows / Ye have little
& left her rolling her eyes
First in rage, then bored, then
          like a saint rolls her eyes up to heaven
                    bold enough to nod to her reflection
          when god was nowhere
                    to be found

"Discovery" in 16th century Europe—tucked away faith instead of making it flagrant; scientific secrets surfaced, opaque or translucent; found loopholes in the Church's law;

Come home to me; inquiring inquisitor; what century holds you together; Or—discovery matched doctrine, afraid to dispute it; (it must be so if they tell me so);

De revolutionibus oribum coelestium, the revolution of *heavenly* spheres; geocentric-turned-heliocentric; printing press, gunpowder, compass;

A revolutionary effort resists both shame and the urge to inhabit it;

Both *did I do that* and *what have I done*; to upset you?

As if the bifurcation of you, a you split in two, becomes dissonant bells ringing at once and in your ears—*am I this*—and *how am I immune*—to what is known?

A dissected frog is an example of a poet, to teenage scientists;

The surrealist artist Max Ernst wrote as a motto for his novel-in-drawings, *Une Semaine de Bonté,* "And I object to the love of ready-made images in place of images to be made."

Heléne Cixous writes through Promethea, "I dread nothing as much as autobiography. Autobiography does not exist. Yet so many believe that it exists."

As a teen I thought the miracle of my body was bleeding every month without dying;

A miracle of inking blank pages without dying—reigning space without dying, then calling it a colony. Does the book follow this formula?

In a book collecting Jenny Saville's museum-sized enorms of painted bodies; paint used as flesh, a subject, and not the other way around; she says, "...the use of bodies to embody an idea."

I'd rather ideas infused their flesh like collagen puffs the lips; the lips are arguments that set the course for centuries of empirical understanding; What century; what lips; O;

The mouth, the way Caspar Bartholin (1585-1629) swore the unicorn's existence and dismissed the doubting Thomases of the Ptolemaic world—

blessed are those who do not yet see;
Desiring a genus that might also include the rhinoceros and the
monocerous—
blessed are those who inherit the earth;
So that any single-horned animal might belong together in concept; a
beatitude;
Intaglio carved out of flesh—is a poem a machine or a machine's antidote?
A scratch—reveals this logic: what I can't be sure exists—exists to fill what
I suspect about it; *blessed are those who mourn—blessed are those who are
reviled;*
So that I can demonize or demarcate what is not understood—in the interest
of keeping the peace—to understand myself alone; a geocentric pill in the
stitching.

A pill in stitching ought to be plucked out, states the logic of lint removers, where frictions pose obstacles to the smoothness of sweaters;

The expense of the sweater is related to the number of pills; the population of pills to be meted out; the expense of the fibers of the hair make the value of the sweater;

By the pills it will not have;

What pills made possible, in art and life, was bleeding without dying;

By pills it will not swallow; *swallow swallow,* says the sun, who creates the conditions for pills and their possible chemistries as medicine, mendicant, mediocre food;

Upon pondering the pill clears the migrainal confusion; writing becomes lucid again; sentences end;

If by pill I mean something which alters an internal state to make its sphere of influence more bearable; something which enhances it;

Something which, appended to a suffix, -age, creates conditions of forced evacuation;

I dutifully explain the lazy pill as one which accepts its conditions for knowing no alternative; a pill without imagination;

The treatment of conditions as either *no big deal* or which are such a big deal that they cannot be dealt with, per se, without first destroying thee;

Misdiagnosis of the present, a wandering womb;

This book began as a study of matter and ephemera in terms of occluded archives; what gets surfaced; what gets stolen;

What gets treated as an object and what stays, after having been made one by the weather or culture;

the sweaterdom condition and the lack of heart at the middle of it, at finding the conditions to be itchy, impossible;

I thought or think of life as an atmosphere, a climate that, if it is to be weathered at all, might by strong bases; not tall orders;

All hands; but what, as a poet, do I know;

In the writing each of us appears ineffectual and maybe I feel it this way; the performance; the desire to authenticate without a password reset; the lack, maybe, of suitable suitors or an inability, maybe, to make oneself suitable to others;

A chronicle of tensions; pills in the relational fabric; doozies of metaphor and making-object out of what refuses to be such in body;

I impossible object; this recognition makes theory of matter untenable; disproves a hypothesis; misread misthread;

That if one can carve out time and all possible stipulations for objecthood, it will be possible to perform oneself as such; the failure to be or act toward an object reveals, in the writing, opacities coming to light; a mind at odds with itself;

A love letter written in the present, so that love itself might not be conditional upon the whims of its past or future tense.

I am not convinced I am not a letter; mere interface with data imports;

but I am convinced the force behind it is miscalculated; I am convinced love is an inadequate word that I weaponize;

De mortuis nil nisi bonum; do not speak ill of the dead;

I weaponize it because love is a power of the utterer; love love love love; *ow ow ow ow;*

It makes weather;

And because of this, I can't answer: what is it to survive if preserving one's life means annihilating its conditions? (How can I live like this?);

Which tries to answer the epigraph, *what is more real, the sculpture, or the stone that's cut away?*

And in some way answers, is the birth scream of my mother sunk somewhere in my bones?

Between a memorial or the luxury of forgetting; like the estate which, vacated by the dead, sells their belongings in an auction sale;

De mortuis nil nisi bonum; what's uttered in their absence; what stands in for them;

Hoarders, collectors of ephemera that is not ephemera at all, reveal that in death, objects are really little more than food;

Object [from Medieval Latin objectum: thing presented to the mind]

I equate the writing with an object, though it comes from me, an animal, in a way that feels like radio blood; all the ambience in the typed-out chillwave and cat snores;

Carnivorous reader, perhaps it feels natural to you to eat me;

It was not to me; between the first time I wrote this book and now, the writing and I had a feud; I read myself, then—I lacked "weight," I lacked "substance";

Or—I contained too much of each, and escaped my own grasp—I lost sight of "reality"; Became unfathomable benthic beatitude;

I wanted to examine matter and memory in terms of a body and the ephemera passing through it on any given day;

Ventriloquize the ethnomusicologist and his scratched pots; listen for masters;

But the art of theory is not divisible by the narration of the past, nor its absence;

It is an act of control (of this landscape);

After many months of revision, during which I could only think to delete the original and start over—razing the landscape of the page—raising the dead; I lay down on my belly, defeated on the couch;

Sighing, I apologized to the absence; I apologized for the accumulation of the past as I tried to surrender to its sculpture, the desire to be preserved; This was months before R said *we should go our separate ways,* when he stroked my hair and said *don't try to rewrite the past*—but I thought, what else can I do?

Taina Bruguera states in her "Manifesto on Artists' Rights," *Art is a way of building thought, of being aware of oneself and others at the same time. It is a methodology in constant transformation in the search for a here and now.* I wanted to explain the uncut jade in terms of its shards because I was afraid of the shards;

Of recreating the conditions for its shatter; its glass *fati*;

In the way Woodbridge thought he heard the word *blue* being spoken in his ancient pots;

So song lyrics became earworms in de-compositions of essays; (in the revision, I mostly cut them out, because they do not belong to me);

But surrounded me; defined me by accretion; my Kuiper belt, for me, their planet; what is this dark matter; decay?

How L asked when I went home to record voices: *do I want anything in the house?*

Like Voyager's golden record of earth's sounds; do I want a scratch of song? The landfill of objects fooling me into thinking I am not one;

A piano we crowded around to warble O You Beautiful Doll;

White couch that only jams the emptiness of the room; no one dares dirty it;

A painting by a distant relative—someone of some talent, who copied Vermeers and died in the war—or at least we heard he died in the war, someone knew him, they saw him tossed-out in the trenches, it was a classic war story...?

The lampshade that, when lit, formed a houndstooth pattern bloating open in parabolas on the wall;

these forgotten files in the basement cabinets, this unused ukulele, a box of Metlife desk calendars from 1999; spoon collection; Doilies;

A handful of porcelain salt shakers of white women in pinafores stacked alongside miniature gangs of cocker spaniels, whose expressions, if they did not intend to communicate to the human their consciousness, served as reminder of his own.

[TAG 15]
archeologists distill a woman

                                        Rotting in the mountains
I am the reliquary I am the reliquary

triste, tristes, tristeza /
                    The Kitchen Maid (c. 1658), The Music Lesson (c. 1662-65),
                    The Girl with a Pearl Earring (c. 1665-66)

                    religion

        border, bang bang
bulb held in abeyance
by gods who dangle planets
                    like a mobile over a cribbed baby

GLASS *FATI* _____
           (smoothed)

The Iceman thaws in Italy;

For a nomad, an object does not indicate origin so much as serve as the source of her diffusion;

A magnifying glass zooms in at the rate of my reading comprehension;

Ice thaws and I imagine it functions like eyeware; clarifying what it thaws to be what it is: a thing-in-itself; to trust?

Scraping the goop and smashing linoleum onto canvas; well-designed;

Here I am in the present; 5,000 years ago a man, now dissected, reveals the pollen in his belly from hop hornbeam blossoms that fell through the wind onto his food;

I make equations of person, color, element, year; accidental gardens; spiced ice; the melt—uncurtains the sculpture—the melt asks;

What are you even doing here?

What C said amidst the karaoke last night; maybe we were a little drunk;

We'd commandeered the one soft place in the room;

I joy-goggled—Iceman was old by then, at 40, wearing bearskin soles; he kept a flint-tipped dagger and a copper-bladed ax, some embers wrapped in maple leaves and birchbark, an unfinished longbow and quiver;

I'd fixated on a man, 40, who danced by himself with one finger pointed at the ceiling, wagging it smiling, his eyes shut;

Iceman was murdered 5,000 years ago; he was running away;

They know because he went into the wilderness unarmed, and died there;

Bar man spit on me by accident; he said things like "it's our generation that's doing it, right here, in Logan Square!" or "I saw Arthur Miller's last play right before he died!"

I could not answer so I went to the bathroom;

Scientists see the isotopes in Iceman's teeth and in his bones and they know where he lived and where he ran;

They cut into his intestines to find some mica he ate in stone-ground grain;

So I know C was right when she said I snub; I turn away; she said *I don't think you try to hurt people but your own means of self-preservation ends up hurting*;

I said I didn't understand;

What there is of me to preserve, if I turn away to preserve something;

Is it truer to say I self-abnegate; turn back toward not-knowing; before threads of thought turn fragile or frayed, and get confusing;

A scientist takes Iceman's hand in hers and knows, from feeling his brittle fingernail, he'd been chronically ill;

Another concludes his last meal was red deer;

Have I pricked you with a needle to make a cut or mend one?

I said to C *I'm so tired of feeling foamy*; the foam my condition; the foam begat a self skimming the foam with her teeth; to cut the foam, to live a foamless life is more "present," whatever that means;

I told C I wanted to be more present;

Though I write that and it feels like I lie; I am not careless; but the foam makes it look that way, like cappuccino foam deceives the drinker into liquid; like seafoam deceives the thinker into debris; like a philosopher is deceived into writing the foam; as poets are deceived into thinking that etymological excavation is philosophy;

An archaeobotanist sees the einkorn, wheat and barley mixed with charcoal, and can tell that he ate bread;

When I tell you what I "know," I hardly know what I'm saying;

She identifies 80 species of moss and liverworts around him, knows where he hid in the mountains, had chosen to leave the deciduous for the coniferous and left it for the deciduous again, then stopped;

I think about myself in the third person; the foaminess of affective conditions outside my control; on a plane; at-large; how much money in my bank account;

the contagious feels of culture; virtual petri;

I think: she is a fiction; she thinks therefore she is a fiction; she is—

Something that does not belong to herself, but scientists in a far future;

"Mattering," in the sense of organ donation; machinic utility; worker bee;

The snub is a pivot where I recognize this self-turned-fiction; recognizing that the other thinks otherwise of you; where I become aware of, say, fathoms in myself;

A greenish-yellow turned the darker algaeic colors of hadal, benthic zones; where electric nervous systems wear sleeves of fish who don't care that they're ugly;

A fathom is an act of grasping;

So that when another gets close to me, says "I miss *you,* I love *you,* I want, desire, *you*"; bruising the skin between art and tool;

I grasp at possible explanations; self-knowing my body as their object;

Relations by which the statement might appear *logical* & not *suspect*; birth scream in my bones;

A claim that is not fair for me to question, because it is a feeling that belongs to another; a bruise pulsing neonly to warn me;

This separation; how do I know; *how can I live like this?*

Or recognition that the feeling is not held in space (& thus discernible) but contained within a body (& thus outside my grasp); word-without-word;

Yet reflected at me like I *should know, ought to know;* not-alone;

This moment C called the snub, the turning away; a moment of disembodiment; the moment I am given to myself as a lie; *Oh fuck Vör that is some patriarchal bullshit;* or its tenet technocracy; the only preposition that accompanies capitalism is *under;*

Spouted like a whale's exhale; when they're stressed their cortisol levels rise too; drones fly through the blow with petri dishes to measure them;

A scientific object makes another possible; a badly-written one is pseudo;

Scientists found the outline of an arrow in Iceman's breast; can they tell if he reached for the hole?

[TAG 16]

Fear of being buried alive: *taphophobia*

Left behind, forgotten: *athazagoraphobia*

Magic: *rhabdophobia*

Deadlines: *ergophobia*

Fear, wishes: *phobophobia*

Thunder, lightning: *astraphobia*

Fire: *pyrophobia*

Dreams: *oneirophobia*

She appeared alive after 1500 years of entombment; Tullia, daughter of
Cicero, incorruptible *pietá triste tristes triesteza*;
found alongside a lamp that had also been burning since; John Donne called
it a love-lamp;
I think: I *is* a fiction; like Rimbaud's assertion *je suis autre;* to question the
"realness" of the I is to accept its lie, translated as those sci-fi vids from the
80s that show a human head enframed in technicolor regress to infinity;
How success is measured at the rate of dehumanization?
As if we arise from ambivalence, a confusion of "who I am" and not "what is
it I belong to, and what is the force of its conditions?"
I'm not writing anything new, these days, to be honest I do not think about
this question; rather *who is it I must become* (in order to survive the space
where I find myself);
Is this because I am female-bodied; do I think in terms of my body's
potential to host; of its subsequent destruction and transformation?
Because, if I am good enough, I might join the ranks of saints and Eva Perón,
incorrupt and sleeping beauty, in a clear coffin, as an example to the rest of
them?
Now, having landed, again, I realize that it is because the axiom is not *I think
therefore I am,* nor *I think therefore I doubt that I am* but *I am a fiction;*
Tale of possible performance; what Hito Steyerl calls a "proxy," decoy;
stand-in; a ventriloquist doll of oneself; withdrawing from a present that
demands her attention;
It is not said whether Tullia reeked of peonies, a telltale sign of sainthood;
in fact, not much is known about her life as a subject of her own life; she is a
snippet of others; Daughter of Cicero, wife of Frugi, wife of Crassipes, wife
of Dolabella, mother of his two sons, one who died the year he was born, the
other whose birth killed her;
Catholic saints and beatis need neither ice nor formaldehyde to look alive,
because their souls, so pure, bypass putrefaction;
Though I walk through the uncanny valley as an anachronism, this does not
make everyone else real: everyone else becomes a fiction, too;

Masks are selves; the fiction is a weapon; a method of attaining power;
Uttering a word; like once, below the parish, corpses drained out over
meshed toilets in a spa called a putredarium—until just the bones lay on the
trays;

A physical corollary to spiritual purgatory;

Where priests said mass for the souls, whose families witnessed their slow
decay over the course of a year or so; then stored the bones, purified of flesh,
in an ossuary while the soul went off, cleansed, to heaven;

Egypt began embalming to make a body into a hard mask; decomposing
flesh is insufficient architecture for runaway souls;

When I talked about an ex I said *we needed each other to be perfect objects,
but we were the exact opposite;*

C said that's the first line of a book; I said oh no; that to write myself as a
fiction might mean catharsis or cathexis, but what cycle do I repeat on the
way?

Upon discovery that some bodies do not rot—or that chemicals lining the
coffin perform an accidental kind of embalming—the church confirmed the
body's sainthood; incorruptibility a guarantee of sinlessness;

How will I know when the cycle's been completed; once I say the word or
write the story;

What secret will I live then?

Nuns placed the saint in a glass case, or severed her hands and made them
into relics, or fashioned a wax face over her drying one; the faithful came
in droves to further adorn her with peony-wreaths and votive gifts or
sanctuary lamps;

Elizabeth Wagner writes that witnessing a loved one's fleshy decomposition
from familiar face to anonymous bones acclimates the family to loss, and
eventually, to accept it.

[TAG 17]

                              that we are fooled
by decoy migration roosts
Virga virgin vag—none of these touch

[TAG 18]

As nature giveth and taketh away, sudden or slow death / dead girl is a good
girl

[TAG 19]

[TAG 20]
incorruptible Eva

[TAG 21]

Sweet-smelling things
                    Sour in rarefied air

                              [TAG 22]
What body lies buried in the sand or ice
& what killed
          & what got left
(do you remember

VOLCANO CLOTHES _____

(aporia)

A diffuse object is a forever fiction; sand-combing every a.m. a new pattern;
I sit in N's studio leafing through her art books while she works on a
drawing; Mannerism; Max Ernst; Jenny Saville—who talks about paint like
flesh, her subjects as enlivened flesh, bodies, simply, the paint exaggerating
this quality of life in flesh and not the image-factory within it; Saville is
quoted,

"When I was painting the genital area, I was trying to think about ways to
use intense color to make marks that heightened the feeling of sex. Then
when I painted the thigh, I had this area at the topside of the thigh and had
four or five tones mixed up that I knew I wanted to run into each other. I got
them all really oily."

The interviewer asks her, *What is your aim actually?*

Jenny says, *I want it to be acute.*

Like a poem? Interviewer asks again. Jenny replies, "*—trying to get to it—to
suck it out of yourself and out of the painting, there is a moment it starts to
breathe...*"

My infinity regress means I keep rewriting my finished product;

To protest my deadness; I conceive the appropriate death for a posthumous
life;

Doing what the wind does in the desert—fossilizing forms, preserving what
remains in an eons-long process of blowing;

I the ego-long regency; blue blue blue blue bloody;

How early Egyptians buried their dead in sand; the body fetal, in linen,
stucco molded around it;

Stan Brakhage's *The Act of Seeing With One's Own Eyes* spends 32 minutes
in a morgue—no sound, no narration, no faces;

Except those being peeled from their flesh;

Where the Egyptians fashioned a mask so the dead person's soul, or *ba,*
might recognize its former body in the tomb and return to carry it along the
road to immortality—they burst into a star;

In the morgue, forensicists peel to reveal the meat beneath; clinical
measures of the ribs, the neck, the penis make the peeling more efficient;

The mini buzzsaw pops off the skull for brain examination; I am aware;
Squeamishness prevents me from appreciating the film; partly about the
body itself and the way it is treated, in death, as a thing;
I am aware that critique comes from fear of susceptibility;
A conflict of wanting both my experience and to diagnose it, as if one might
save me from the other; as if diagnosis might spare future generations the
disease;
Craving a better burial, the way rich Egyptians craved a better burial, and so
built tombs called *mastabas* to protect themselves from the wind and sand;
Inciting decomposition; inviting mummification, drying the body with
natron salt; do I desire the acute life or a *long dureé?*
Because the rich got richer, *mastabas* became for pharaohs only, which
the poor spent their lives building; ensuring an afterlife for the rich whilst
denied a life of their own;
Crowding the dead with rote, nonfiction objects.

Neither science nor art saves a dysphoric species from its emergencies; e.g.,
a sociopathic cinema makes a museum of the senses, an amputation;
R and I watched Stan Brakhage again in the theater with a hundred others,
in silence; their coughs and shuffles and laughter chafed, turned flatulent;
But not like in a church, where the body ends in shame; rather, the films
without sound did not elaborate on this absence;
Ahem, *scuff-scuff, ha ha ha*; no sonic response from the film, it told us to *cut
it out;* so we resented sharing the space with the offenders;
The way children in a library will *shhh* their comrades to avoid collective
punishment;
R put his hand to his forehead as he does when the outer world becomes
unbearable in its wrongness, in the stupidity of others who do not
recognize its wrongness and continue to participate without the righting
of acetic refusal, the only appropriate answer to a world overstuffed by its
infringement on others;
How long will this go on? Ferreting out 'signals' in the 'noise'?
Amputating sound did not comment on the deaf, nor inspire a narrative—
The habit of the mind without accompaniment;
Our shared amputation and its subsequent isolation; *shhh*;
Its alienating chill, as on Everest; where dead hikers are landmarks for those
still determined to summit, despite;
If I don't like what I've written it is usually a tense issue; marking things
in time or space makes it stale or makes decay impossible; I mean to make
colors bleed, as a water-soluble painting; or decomposing roadkill;
Cool air kept the murdered Iceman captive for millennia: space as prison;
soundlessness as its reminder;
Stan Brakhage did not make a mask for himself, but gave the audience
a mask—his/camera's eyes flutter in beats twice that of memory, thrice
breathing, there is no body in it, despite;
To be given a mask, in numbers, is to be made-machine; made-object; made-
thing;
Can you hear the makers—without engine? Silencer; noise-cancelling;

Does it speak to you?

As hikers summit, they reach a point where they are "actively dying," where the altitude is high enough that they must survive on supplemental oxygen; the body begins its countdown there;

We didn't last; many walked out;

I tried to stay, but R sighed because a drunk man kept laughing, inserting his glee incongruently with the screen for which he was the sole reactor; & I cringed at the attention, on screen, to cops, given the same sensitive shots as the children in the short film that preceded it;

I whispered *do you want to go* and we did;

Often the oxygen runs out; climbers risk death if they try to bring a body back; they sign a waiver expressing what to do with their bodies if they die; At around $30,000 to helicopter the body out, most accept that if they fall, if an avalanche hits, or if they run out of breath, the body belongs to the air; They will not dissolve, but they will freeze, forever cleaving to the mountain they loved enough to risk their lives;

How dare he make a story of me; how dare my body entropy and confetti in this space of brutal arrhythmic montage; how dare the gaze rob the substance of me, who paid nothing to see it but bought the book anyway; Over 200 bodies mark the passage as neon omens, reminding followers of failure and fragility in bold trekking boots and blue down jackets;

R said *I think I died on the peak;* he meant the virtual has stolen his political agency, that, since politics is largely relegated to its consumption by media, he doesn't think he can be part of a major labor movement anymore, *it's just the way it is;*

Fiction is not always freeing, in the sense of escape, or empathy as a vehicle for inhabitations elsewise; its imposition on you implies you are not given a choice to be yourself, to own your experience, to choose death;

You belong to the mountain, enslaved to it, in the opposite way Adrienne Rich writes of women mountaineers:

The cold felt cold until our blood / grew colder   then the wind / died down and we slept;

At lower altitudes, the earth is an ossuary, claiming the flesh while the bones
remain;

How an overperformance of an emotion can diminish its violence; then to
assume the earth conspires with it;

*What does it mean   "to survive" / A cable of blue fire ropes our bodies /
burning together in the snow*

We will not live / to settle for less   We have dreamed of this / all of our lives.

[TAG 23] when you told me, it felt holy (*amor fati*)

Still, I do not disappear despite new forms.

Do I make you a fiction? As if the assumption in that statement is that I am real, that our relation must be one or the other;

That we are two and that to say "she" in reference to myself requires slicing myself in two;

to cut you off; to cut it out, in terms of the sound I make as I utter it; *woo woo woo woo;*

The colors that appear when I think about this book, and writing it; Adamantine spar, blue blue blue blue, a bruising pink and a crystalline gray ice; a melted bronze shaping itself into a state of vehemence, No, it says, it stabs me the way I am stabbed when I kiss R and he says he *doesn't really like kissing that much,* the needle rubbing one out in the bathtub as it struggles to hear the sound of its conception; am I a made-thing; "real"?

The irony of the other who treats you like a human but does not desire you as an animal nor object, as you desire it;

Visiting the souvenir of the real, if the real was *just a feeling;*

Object Our Lady of Lourdes, a shrine to the venerated Blessed Mary honoring apparitions said to have occurred in Lourdes, France in 1858;

Are you a pilgrim to my souvenirs and relics left behind on your soul's sojourn to verify this realness; to get what you need; a twist in this plot of inquisition;

Millions of Catholics go expecting miracles, to come away changed, to begin a journey at its destination; to be healed;

They find a grotto diorama, where a plastic Mary towers over a diminutive plastic St. Bernadette; *come home to me—*

The souvenirs enact the apparitions that came to Bernadette when she was just 14, 17 apparitions in total, most when Bernadette was fetching water or firewood;

But how did she look to you? They asked, and she described the apparition as she, herself, looked: short-statured and wearing a school uniform; a reflection.

In her devotion, Bernadette sliced herself in two, because a saint is a woman who has cut off her breasts—lead bells, her breasts lead bells;

Preventing that one might torture her out of heresy; you are not allowed to spout fiction, but we can canonize you if we can't prove you wrong;

It is important for saints to find others like them, so they don't get caught up in themselves;

I don't really like kissing that much; become lead; mummified;

What witness, if the witness chooses to demarcate the other in light and air? *To the gods they made / woo woo woo woo;* if the accumulation comes to a consensus, that you are unreal?

As a conspiracy of truths will turn an innocent into a scapegoat—avalanched; she picks at her skin, a mask no soul recognizes; learning to see oneself as such;

Kids play saint after evening mass, one streetlight; in church clothes; stained glass making testimony of interior degradation and vaginal architecture;

An imagination whose language is mosaic forced into words; straight lines itch;

ow ow ow ow;

A child turns away from it, instead sprints toward the streetlight, tosses "I love you, I love you!" like reins of a 19th century buggy, while those who follow bless her mistake, throwing grass that is pretend holy water, muttering to each other and her rabid ghost *you are now in heaven as on earth. Your life begins, Bernadette.*

[TAG 24]

[TAG 25]

[TAG 26]
Aria arrrrrrrraaaahhhhiiiaaaaa
                    A remoter island of a grass god)

[TAG 25]
snap snap / ooooo ow / aaarrrgh / halleeee / heeeellll / hhaallelluujiaaaaaah
snap snap snap

The sun sees itself twice; once androgyne in a microscope; second as aesthete in a palette of promethean hues, unbodied;

Like a graphic novel unfurls in stutters that do not correspond to the eye's management of movement I assume my search for images is in service to a story, but that the story itself is shattered;

Its timing is off; its scale is off; the drawing is dense and *there's just so much going on;*

N teaches her students not to draw things, but the relationships among them;

A collection of microscope slides which, by magnifying the ordinary, both dwarfs the human scale as it makes its macrocosm a sharable thumbnail;

I the bifurcated performance of a shattered eye; half-fig with a wasp in my side; prism-thinking;

Of microscope slides of tears; Rose-Lynn Fisher's photographs of these slides and their varying composition, named by the human experience behind them; *Topography of Tears,* e.g., "What it looked like after a time forgotten," "The irrefutable," "Timeless reunion (in an expanding field)," "In the end it didn't matter," "Tears for those who yearn for liberation," "Tears of elation at a liminal moment" (c. 2013-16).

Elsewhere, another denuded landscape waits to be filled in;

Outside of Overton, Nevada, on the eastern edge of the Mormon Mesa, where the dynamics of a desert valley obscure its identifiable features as much as they inspire visions where there are none;

Michael Heizer's *Double Negative* refocuses scale: the deposition of the natural valley that separates the piece, and the man-made trenches that lie like two innocuous and empty graves on either bank;

The wind blows dust to fill in Heizer's trenches; in an aerial photo *Double Negative* looks like two slashes in skin;

If you were the one floating above the valley with this camera, you might imagine the trenches and the valley make a mold the shape of an overturned *ankh*;

Ankh as in Egyptian tomb paintings, gripped in the hands of gods and goddesses as they bestow its powers upon a mummy: a blessing of safe passage for the dead;

Ankh as in a belief in eternity, an afterlife (the emancipation from or return to the body) where, if the dead had been properly cared for, its soul might recognize the human it left behind; it means "breath of life"; mask;

A collection of memory-images, improperly ankhed, scrapes at scale;

Likelihood challenged my inventory in if/then statements, which blew through me redly, burning, *am I a person or am I manageable and consistent*, did the pattern disturb as a glitch or something the painting "needed," like a pencil stab or a rip in its fabric, to be "understood"?

The algorithm selects for me my oscillations, whether I magnify or diminish conditions;

No safe passage for the dead if I am its filter; manipulated by the light;

A sky made bluer by red sand; deceived by blue spruce and pinyon pines, sage green enough to suggest that you, too, can absorb so much light without dying;

Deceived by the river, which flows like a lapidary statement through the canyon, *I don't feel there is something missing or at fault with you, I don't feel inhibited or some other compression around you...*

Swallow swallow, says the sun; *but I see how much my lack of physical intimacy is hurting you;*

Double Negative waits to be filled in;

In the days of the Old West, outlaws stashed their kill in the canyon's crevices; the rest searched for the lost where buzzards circled;

Nested dendrites edging outward in electric pulses; euphony does not solve the problem of authorial intrusion or omniscience; kill switch;

I feel I am supposed to relay information, here, instead of new patterns of thinking, those that mimic other arts that do what they are supposed to do, photos and music and films;

Where writing is the excavation and communication of knowledge *about it*; what knowledge; can I ever know something enough to tell its story; to require that it soothe me, because I can be sure that I know it, be certain that this gesture of the hand as it describes an event in the past, before meeting me, is not one that harms me, now, as I note that it seems "out-of-character"? *Double Negative* waits to be filled in;

When it is the material that gives the human his "breath of life," and the material is earth, and the earth appears to suffer, whose side am I on—the artist or his "creator"?

Can I hear the maker making his made-things;

"Computational photography," Steyerl writes, "might flag your debt, play your games, broadcast your heartbeat...The camera turns into a social projector, rather than a recorder."

Telling the world who you are by accretion of the data on your phone;

It seems unnatural—to carve into what you want to conserve, to take a piece or pic of what you love and to leave it there, wounded, as a gaudy testimony to loss;

Did Heizer uproot what takes so long to grow out there?

I know that an apology and a relaying of feelings and thoughts is not a magic wand; I understand if you need more time to process, I just wanted to let you know where I'm at;

And natural, all the same; unearth and bury; cut and carve and dam and destroy; leave and let live; divide and conquer;

Double Negative waits to be filled in; bruise cut out of the desert's peeled off skin;

I say nothing because it feels like I can't; feels like something will say so for me; feels like I ought to be a witness to the silence dividing two hurt spaces rather than disrupt the silence by saying they are there;

You can step into the trench of *Double Negative;* you can let the grave swallow you as you look off across the desert valley to see its identical twin, open, its walls seized by the weight of space between you, your apparent insignificance, your body hidden in the larger schemes of creation and destruction by the weather and by men;

Heizer has said, "I guess I'd like to see art become more of a religion";

He wants the piece to go untouched by people until the wind fills the trench again.

[TAG 26]

> Who gets to play artist/god
> one palette edge on another /

    smelly reams of yellowed galactic bruises
mushrooms sprouting in the fungal heap
of the sloughed off context / what subsides

(ombligo   ((ink

RAZE/RAISE _____
        (pink habits)

Loss waters mowed tulips as the Ice Maiden and the Iceman say: ice makes
a person into a cubed museum of all-natural matter; amber, memory; genetic
muck;
Of attachments to familiar faces or anonymous bones;
Tales of fragility; do not trust its rooms and the haze in it; crystal clear, this
groove;
Scratch—(I do not belong to me); memory collects;
like liquid in a coulander—a molecule here and there cometing the dome;
like gossip we share on Insta; this call is a bruise;
(I dip into your barrel with a can to water the hollyhocks and tulips that
grow along the house); the writing is synesthesia;
In 1990 I was three and my mother hated that the tulips grew behind the
house and not in front of it, so uprooted their perennial transgressions;
Come home to me; to the gods we made / woo woo woo woo
When I ask my mother why, she seems surprised; *I don't think I would've
done that*; but I testify; this call is a bruise;
she then uprooted the pine tree in front of the house, replanting it on the
other side of the lawn; ice melts into lawn; paint swills its palette becoming
word become flesh; *what are you even doing here?*
I believed she hated the house and living there, isolated by so much space;
blooms—maybe mocked her imprisonment; to reposition the wilderness
must have felt to her an apt revenge;
Placenta rubbed on a white page; it goes back longer than that; *benandante,
malandante;* relics of inquisitions; woman reliquary; writing;
The scale at which a human-sized hole is seen in the landscape;
Her patience extended to the lilac bushes;
Our oceanic agriculture;
Mowing the lawn without protest from the pines; midwife moo;
If I scratch at thought can I hear her; is the birth scream of my mother sunk
somewhere in my bones?
One day setting fire to the house after two generations growing up in it;
snap snap; triste tristes; yet saving the surrounding trees from immolation;

I do not know why; I condition myself to lose her;

Mold had grown all over the inside; her breasts lead bells; filleted for an audience;

I watched the flames carve out my bedroom window on Facebook; I was twenty, not anywhere near this; imperfect object;

Topography of tears; preserved; amber blood drops with mosquito;

area hemmed-in by sanctification; with the trees *over there* instead of *over here*;

Churning up pop songs in a syncretic fever; *I think I died on the peak;* dying by what she hunts; fearful;

Paint its flesh its flames leave an altar for old trees in a new home, a reassigned territory; caul caterwauling cauterized; snap;

Pushed out, pushed out, go down, Moses, *don't you draw the queen of diamonds, boy / she'll beat you if she's able.*

Does it speak to you?

*

*

un uhn un un un
tangled umbilical / blood
baby baby oh
*

*

*

*

*

*

prima materia—bruises—bodies blueing—ephemeris—epidermis—earworms:

Richard Woodbridge III, "Acoustic Recordings from Antiquity"; The Rolling Stones, "Sympathy for the Devil"; Boyz to Men "End of the Road"; Werner Herzog, *Encounters at the End of the World*; Al Stewart, "Antarctica"; Jason Anthony, "The East Antarctic and the Emptiness Within: Impermanence"; Anais Nin; Pierre Bordieu; Arjun Appadurai; Stuart Hall; Martin Heidegger; Max Ernst, *Une Semaine de Bonté;* Jenny Saville; Taina Bruguera, "Manifesto on Artists' Rights"; Hito Steyerl, *Duty-Free Art;* Elizabeth Wagner, "All the Saints You Should Know"; Stan Brakhage; Steven Hall, "Last Hours of the Iceman"; Caspar Bartholin, *The History of Magic;* Adrienne Rich, "Phantasia for Elvira Shatayev"; *The Song of Bernadette;* Rose Lynn Fischer, "Topography of Tears"; Michael Heizer; *Go Down Moses* is an American spiritual; The Eagles, "Desperado."

ACKNOWLEDGMENTS

With gratitude for characters who appear in this work with altered initials, R, N, C, L—your conversation, presence, art and questions created the writer. For those who held tight while I rewrote, especially Adrian, you lifted the baby out.

Selections from *OMBLIGO/INTAGLIO* appeared in *Minor Literatures* and *BOAAT*. Many thanks to editors Yanina Spizzirri and Sean Shearer.

ABOUT THE AUTHOR

Vör Götte is a stage name of Megan Jeanne Gette, who authored chapbooks *Poor Banished Child of Eve* (H_NGM_N, 2016) and *The Walls They Left Us* (Gloria Anzaldúa Poetry Prize, Newfound, 2016).